10-TASTIC FACTS!

IT TOOK **10 RESEARCHERS** ABOUT **1,525 HOURS** TO FIND THE **3,500 FACTS** IN THE **WEIRD BUT TRUE SERIES.**

WOW!

NATIONAL GEOGRAPHIC
KiDS

weird but true! **10**

350 OUTRAGEOUS FACTS

NATIONAL GEOGRAPHIC
WASHINGTON, D.C.

The average rain

as much as

cloud weighs 100 elephants.

One **spider** species looks like the Hogwarts Sorting Hat in the **Harry Potter** book series.

ANCIENT OCTOPUSES HAD **HARD SHELLS.**

RESEARCHERS CAN TELL WHAT **SHAMPOO** YOU USE BY ANALYZING THE **CHEMICALS** ON YOUR **CELL PHONE.**

7

A U.S. company sells houses you can cover with **flower** and vegetable gardens.

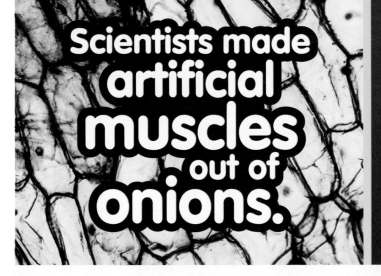

Scientists made **artificial muscles** out of **onions.**

MOSQUITOES PEE ON YOU WHILE **THEY SUCK YOUR BLOOD.**

A **cat** named **Bubba** attends high school in California, U.S.A.

Feline

Bubba

12

A.S.B.

Leland

HIGH SCHOOL

2015 — 2016

Doctors removed a

14-
(6-kg)
pound hair ball from a woman's **stomach.**

AN ICE-CREAM SHOP IN MEXICO CITY, MEXICO, SERVES UP SCOOPS IN DOG-FRIENDLY FLAVORS FOR YOUR PET POOCH.

A **HOUSE** IN NEW YORK, U.S.A., WAS **ENCASED** IN **ICE** DURING A **BLIZZARD.**

brrrrrrr

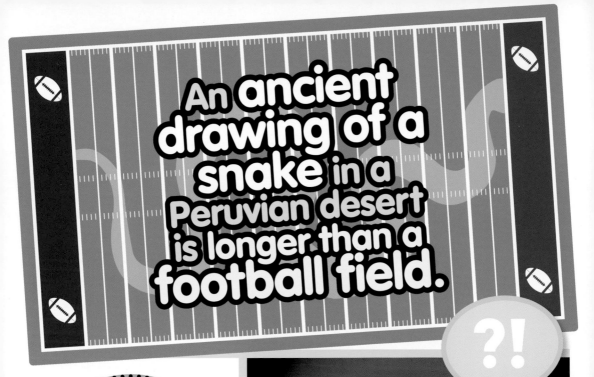

An **ancient drawing of a snake** in a Peruvian desert is longer than a **football field.**

A **BUMBLEBEE** TAUGHT OTHER **BEES** HOW TO MOVE A BEE-SIZE **BALL.**

Scientists have begun to translate bats' language.

?!

IN THE 1800S, PEOPLE OFTEN ANSWERED THE PHONE BY SAYING "AHOY" INSTEAD OF "HELLO."

13

YOU CAN BUY OCTOPUS-FLAVORED POTATO CHIPS.

RAVENS CAN MIMIC HUMAN SPEECH.

FIFTY STRAY CATS

Some **bees** are out cold.

St. Louis, Missouri, U.S.A., went from Spanish to French to U.S. rule in 24 hours.

meow

LIVE ON A HOUSEBOAT
IN AMSTERDAM, NETHERLANDS.

AN ARCHITECT IN TEXAS, U.S.A.,
BUILT A HOUSE
SHAPED LIKE A
COWBOY
BOOT.

ARMADILLOS CAN HOLD THEIR **BREATH** FOR AS LONG AS **SIX MINUTES.**

SHREWS EAT ALMOST NONSTOP.

On average, there are **131 spiders** on every square meter of Earth. (10.8 sq ft)

There are more **book titles** on Earth than there are **different species** of living things.

SOME SCIENTISTS THINK NEW ZEALAND IS A MOUNTAIN PEAK ON A GIANT UNDERWATER CONTINENT.

A 16-YEAR-OLD BLACK BELT IN TAE KWON DO SMASHED 111 CONCRETE BLOCKS WITH HIS HEAD IN ABOUT 35 SECONDS.

A man repairing an **antique piano** found valuable **gold and silver coins** hidden inside.

A woman found her missing wedding **ring**— in her **dog's vomit!**

(IT'S BELIEVED THE RING WAS LODGED IN THE DOG'S STOMACH FOR AS LONG AS FIVE YEARS.)

oops!

21

People in Tibet put yak butter in their tea.

THERE IS A HIDE-AND-SEEK WORLD CHAMPIONSHIP.

In Tokyo you can have dinner at a **vampire-themed restaurant** decorated with **skulls** and **coffins.**

Fireflies are really **beetles.**

It can take as long as **two weeks** for a **wombat** to **digest** a meal.

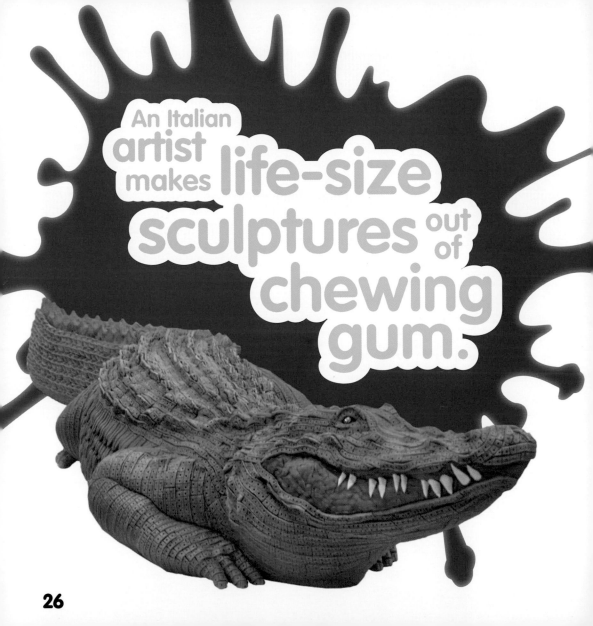

An Italian artist makes life-size sculptures out of chewing gum.

26

ADDING **SALT** TO A **PINEAPPLE** MAKES IT **TASTE** SWEETER.

In 2015, workers repairing a water leak found a time capsule Paul Revere buried in 1795.

SOME **BEES THROW UP** NECTAR TO KEEP THEIR **HEADS COOL** WHILE THEY **FLY.**

A *94-YEAR-OLD WOMAN* IN INDIANA, U.S.A., HAS BEEN WORKING AT THE SAME *MCDONALD'S* FOR MORE THAN *45 YEARS.*

FRENCH BULLDOG

+

PUG

FRUG

29

Lemons float; limes sink.

SCIENTISTS BUILT A $1,000 TREADMILL FOR SHRIMP.

Boaty McBoatface= an underwater research vessel named in an online poll

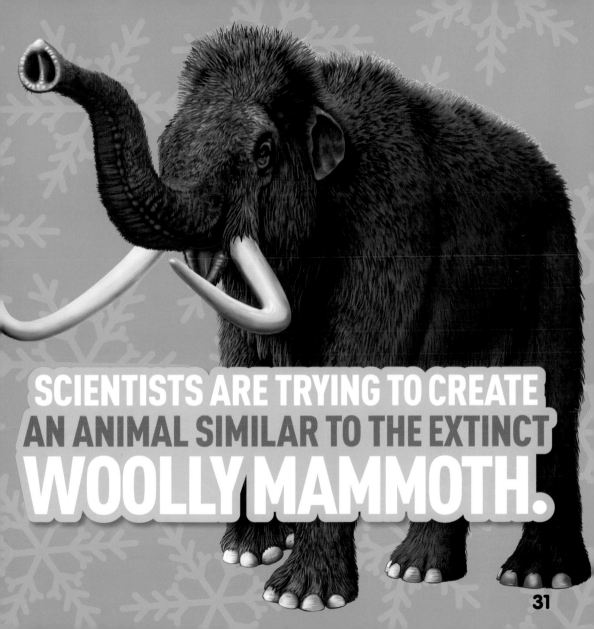

SCIENTISTS ARE TRYING TO CREATE AN ANIMAL SIMILAR TO THE EXTINCT WOOLLY MAMMOTH.

A professional **tennis match** in Florida, U.S.A., was delayed when an **iguana** ran onto the court.

A **PLAYER** IN THE MATCH EVEN SNAPPED A *SELFIE* WITH THE *RUNAWAY* **REPTILE!**

Taking a hot bath can be just as **healthy** as going on a **30-minute walk,** a study shows.

Butter has been around for at least 4,000 years.

MARGARINE WAS DYED PINK TO

THE AVERAGE AMERICAN EATS **5.6 POUNDS** OF **BUTTER** (2.5 kg) A YEAR.

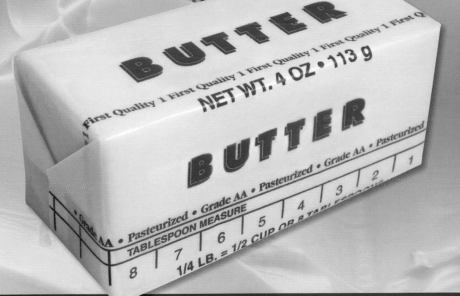

DISTINGUISH IT FROM BUTTER.

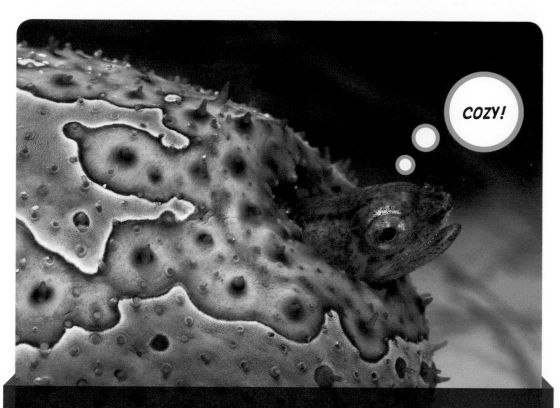

STAR PEARLFISH SOMETIMES LIVE INSIDE
SEA CUCUMBERS' REAR ENDS.

Three billion years ago, a **tsunami** as tall as a **skyscraper** may have swept across **Mars,** scientists believe.

A FIFTH GRADER ONCE TEXTED HER **LOCAL POLICE** DEPARTMENT'S NONEMERGENCY LINE FOR HELP WITH HER MATH HOMEWORK.

You can buy *perfume* that **smells** like kitten fur, popcorn, or earthworms.

THE WORLD'S FIRST SHIP TUNNEL— A MILE-LONG (1.6-km) PASSAGEWAY IN **NORWAY'S** STADHAVET SEA— WILL BE AS TALL AS A 15-STORY BUILDING.

THERE'S AN EMPTY CRYPT **BENEATH THE U.S. CAPITOL BUILDING IN WASHINGTON, D.C.**

SCIENTISTS **STUDY** FOSSILIZED **POOP** TO LEARN WHAT NEANDERTHALS **ATE.**

A group of **rats** is called a **mischief.**

SUDAN HAS MORE

PYRAMIDS THAN EGYPT.

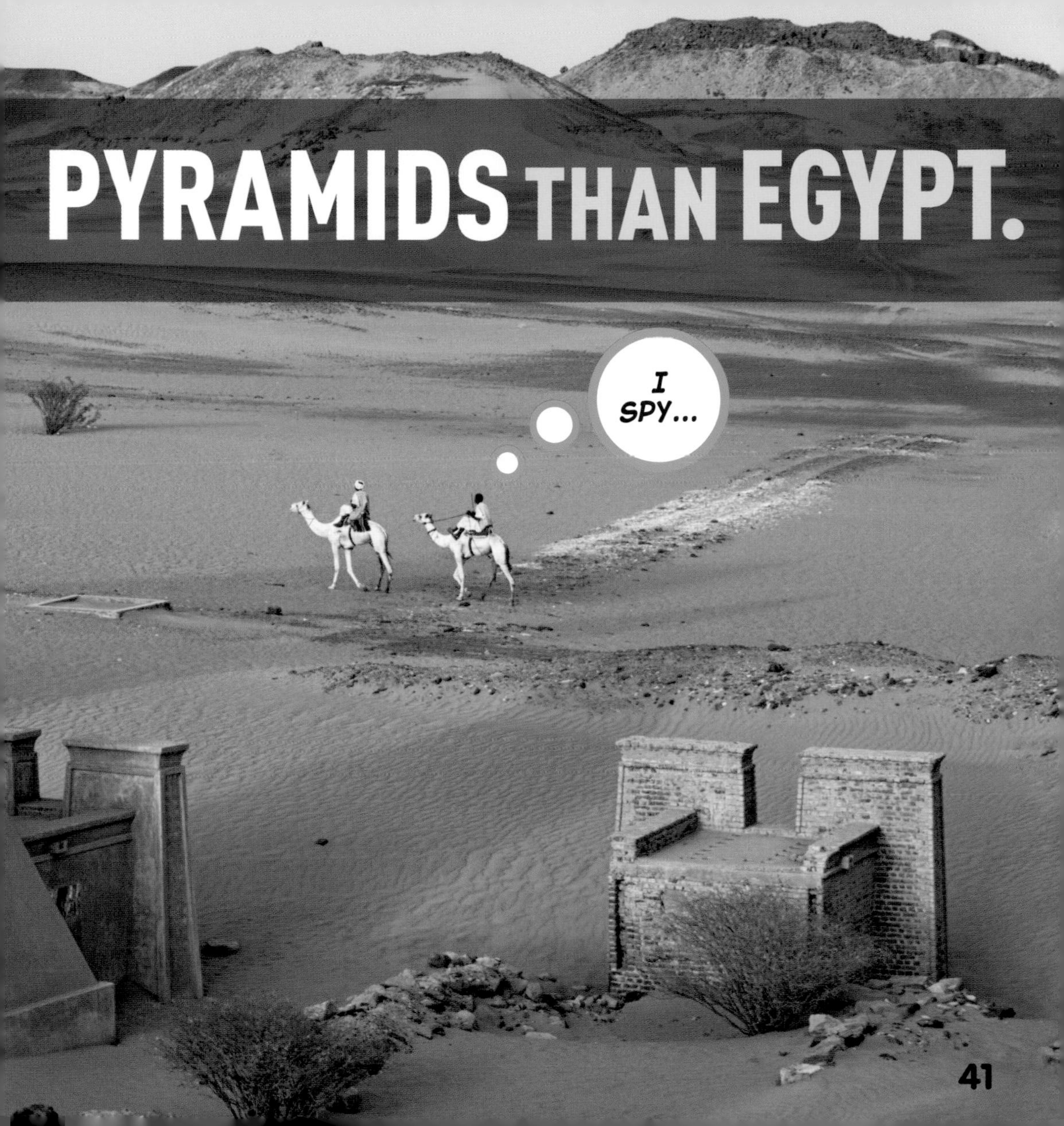

AS PART OF A PROMOTION, A CHICKEN RESTAURANT **ONCE GAVE AWAY FREE FRIED CHICKEN BOUQUETS** ON **VALENTINE'S DAY.**

For about $70, you can send someone *a bouquet of roses made from* **deep-fried bacon.**

THERE ARE **10** TIMES AS MANY **GALAXIES** IN THE **UNIVERSE** AS **SCIENTISTS** PREVIOUSLY THOUGHT.

A British couple spent **10 YEARS** building a model **RAILWAY** throughout their **HOUSE** and garden.

THE **SKINNY HOUSE** IN LONG BEACH, CALIFORNIA, IS ONLY 10 FEET (3 m) **WIDE.**

10 **CONTESTANTS** left in the wilderness for a reality TV show **STAYED FOR A YEAR** before learning that the show had been **CANCELED.**

AS OF 2016, ONLY 10 WOMEN HAD EVER MADE THE FBI'S MOST WANTED LIST.

An **A10**-size piece of paper is **TOO SMALL** to write on.

A **CAR** COMPANY once made a **BOOK** that was **10 FEET** (3 m) **TALL.**

BETWEEN 1993 AND 2013, **10 NEW COUNTRIES** WERE CREATED.

$$1 + 2 + 3 + 4 = 10$$

The Korean alphabet has **10 VOWELS.**

10 POUNDS (4.5 kg) of bat dung was found in an **OFFICE CEILING** in Florida, U.S.A.

10 -TASTIC FACTS!

What? It wasn't just me!

The island of **Sumatra, Indonesia,** is the **only place where tigers, rhinos, elephants,** and **orangutans live together** in a **natural habitat.**

6

A bakery in Missouri, U.S.A., launched a doughnut 97,000 feet into space (29,565 m) using a helium weather balloon.

WITH A "PIE TOP" SNEAKER, YOU CAN ORDER PIZZA BY PRESSING A BUTTON ON THE SHOE'S TONGUE.

A COMPANY IN LOS ANGELES, CALIFORNIA, LIVE STREAMED A RACE BETWEEN A TORTOISE AND A HARE. (THE TORTOISE WON!)

1 2 3 4

Research found that **babies cry more** in Britain, Canada, and Italy than anywhere **else in the world.**

They **cry the least** in Denmark, Germany, and Japan.

At least 18 percent of pet owners **FaceTime** with their furry friends, a recent survey showed.

Baby humpback whales whisper to their mothers.

A SMALL MARBLE COMPASS

ON THE CAPITOL BUILDING'S FLOOR

MARKS THE EXACT **CENTER** OF WASHINGTON, D.C.

The most common color of penguin **poop** is **pink.**

National Animal Crackers Day is on April 18 in the U.S.

51

A PACK OF
WILD
BOARS
WAS
SPOTTED
WANDERING
THE **CITY**
STREETS
IN SOPOT, POLAND.

About **4.5 million** years ago, **raindrops** made ● of **iron** fell on Earth.

You can get a **neck massage** by a **four-foot-long python** at a (1.2-m) **hair salon** in Germany.

THE ISLAND OF MADAGASCAR SMELLS LIKE VANILLA ICE CREAM.

A frog uses its long eyes to help push food down its throat.

THE HAWAIIAN ISLANDS WERE ONCE CALLED THE SANDWICH ISLANDS.

THE AMOUNT OF **LICORICE MADE** IN THE U.S. **EACH YEAR**

A 12-YEAR-OLD BOY WON A ROTTEN SNEAKER CONTEST—AND $2,500—FOR HAVING SHOES THAT REEKED OF POOP AND FISH GUTS.

COULD WRAP AROUND THE EARTH SOME 16 TIMES.

Rats and chimpanzees can laugh.

hahahaha!

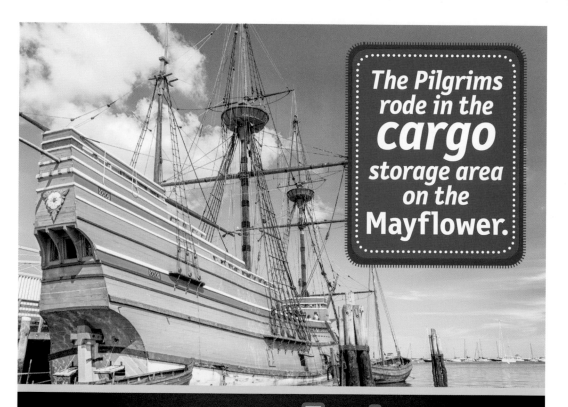

The Pilgrims rode in the **cargo** storage area on the **Mayflower**.

Researchers in **Egypt** found a **3,000-year-old fake toe** attached to a **skeleton's foot.**

THE U.S. MILITARY USED **SLUGS** TO DETECT **LETHAL GAS** DURING WORLD WAR I.

"Beautiful" and *"pneumonia"* are among the most **misspelled words** in the United States, according to a poll.

IN LESS THAN A DAY, A **SINGLE ROBOT** BUILT A **BUILDING** HALF THE SIZE OF THE **U.S. CAPITOL DOME.**

Engineers developed a bacteria-powered battery.

A TIGHTROPE WALKER COOKED AN OMELET OVER **NIAGARA FALLS** AND LOWERED THE DISH TO PEOPLE IN A **BOAT BELOW.**

During the **Vietnam War,** the U.S. used **fake dog poop** as secret **radio transmitters.**

There
are giant
dust
tornadoes
on
Mars.

The **giant Pacific octopus** can have more than **50,000 babies** at one time.

On a hot day, the **Space Needle**, in Seattle, Washington, U.S.A., **expands about one inch.**

(2.5 cm)

THERE IS A **SEED** THAT LOOKS LIKE A HAMBURGER.

BUMBLEBEES CAN RECOGNIZE EACH OTHER BY THEIR SMELLY FOOTPRINTS.

A restaurant in Paris, France, serves food flavored with dirt.

One item on the menu: a stew simmered with mud from the Seine River

THERE ARE **3,000 WORDS** IN THE **KLINGON LANGUAGE.**

YOU CAN LEARN KLINGON—
THE LANGUAGE SPOKEN ON *STAR TREK*— AT A SCHOOL IN SWITZERLAND.

WHILE VISITING THE WHITE HOUSE, BRITISH PRIME MINISTER WINSTON CHURCHILL REPORTED SEEING PRESIDENT LINCOLN'S GHOST.

HENRY VIII OF ENGLAND BANNED MOST CITIZENS FROM PLAYING GAMES LIKE TENNIS, CARDS, AND DICE.

Chicken McNuggets come in just **four shapes:** the ball, the boot, the bell, and the bow tie.

SOME MUSHROOMS CAN MAKE THEIR OWN BREEZE.

Courting **seahorses**
dance together every morning.

NINTENDO started as a playing-card company in 1889.

TERMITES ARE A SOURCE OF METHANE, A GREENHOUSE GAS.

SOME CATS PURR AS MANY AS 150 TIMES PER SECOND.

SNAIL SHELLS WERE ONCE USED AS MONEY.

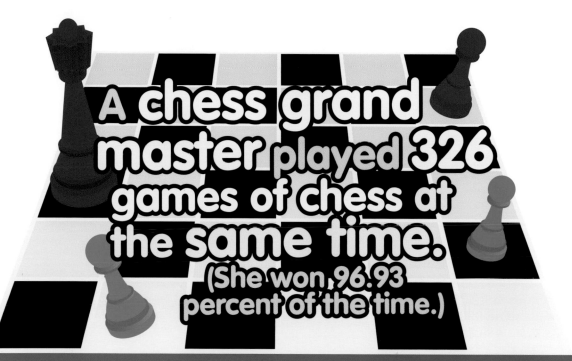

A chess grand master played 326 games of chess at the same time. (She won 96.93 percent of the time.)

ABOUT **100 PEOPLE** COULD FIT INSIDE A **BLUE WHALE'S** MOUTH.

OPOSSUMS ARE ABOUT THE SIZE

OF A GRAIN OF RICE AT BIRTH.

They're so tiny that 14 babies can fit in a teaspoon.

WAX WORM CATERPILLARS EAT PLASTIC SHOPPING BAGS.

A **woman** in Idaho, U.S.A., said **she wrecked her car** because she **saw Sasquatch** alongside the **highway.**

ONE **BRIDE-TO-BE** MADE HER **WEDDING DRESS** ENTIRELY OUT OF **FAST-FOOD WRAPPERS.**

Half of **Earth's** **water** is melted **space ice** that existed before **the sun.**

WOUNDS HEAL TWICE AS FAST **DURING THE DAYTIME** THAN AT NIGHT, ONE STUDY SHOWED.

A TYPE OF **KATYDID** IN SOUTH AMERICA HAS **EARS** ON ITS **KNEES.**

Kindergartners *in New Hampshire, U.S.A.,* *once hosted a* *wedding* *for their* *class* *ducks.*

A group of people in Massachusetts, U.S.A., **knits sweaters** for **chickens** to **wear** in the **winter.**

NASA'S SPACE POOP CHALLENGE OFFERED $30,000 FOR THE BEST WAY TO GET RID OF HUMAN WASTE IN SPACE.

BIG BIRD IS 8 FEET 2 INCHES (2.5 m) TALL—ABOUT THE SAME HEIGHT AS AN OSTRICH.

In **BOWLING,** three consecutive **STRIKES**—all 10 pins knocked down— is called a **"TURKEY."**

A **$10 BILL** has a shorter life span than a **$1 BILL.**

ALEXANDER HAMILTON, whose face is on the U.S. **$10 BILL,** was almost **BROKE** when he died.

A woman made a **DRESS** out of more than **10,000 STARBURST WRAPPERS.**

ONLY **10 PERCENT** OF AN ICEBERG IS VISIBLE ABOVE THE OCEAN'S SURFACE.

Queen Hedwig of Poland was only **10 YEARS OLD** when she was **CROWNED IN 1384.**

An **ARTIST** in Cleveland, Ohio, U.S.A., made a **10-POUND SCULPTURE** (4.5-kg) of basketball superstar **LEBRON JAMES**— out of **dryer lint.**

A Japanese **SPIDER CRAB** known as **BIG DADDY** measured more than **10 FEET** (3 m) **ACROSS.**

The **FIRST SPACECRAFT** to land on a **COMET** journeyed for **10 YEARS** before landing.

A **CRATER** IN SOUTH AFRICA WAS ONCE **10 TIMES** AS WIDE AS THE **GRAND CANYON.**

It takes **10 POUNDS** (4.5 kg) of **GRAIN** to produce **ONE POUND** (453 g) of **BEEF.**

That's Weird! ●●●

A **DOG** fell off his owner's **BOAT** into the ocean— then safely swam **10 MILES** to shore. (16 km)

ONE IN 10 of the **WORLD'S** known species live in the **AMAZON RAIN FOREST.**

85

THERE ARE MORE THAN 60,000 TREE SPECIES ON EARTH.

A library in Iowa, U.S.A., has **more than 4,000 tiny books,** many of which can be read only with a **magnifying glass.**

Someone once stole a **70-pound, $700** (32-kg) **popcorn ball** from a shop in Ohio, U.S.A. (It was later returned.)

IN 1936, A RUSSIAN SCIENTIST BUILT
A COMPUTER THAT RAN ON WATER.

The song "Mary Had a Little Lamb" is based on a true story.

OSCAR THE GROUCH USED TO BE ORANGE, NOT GREEN.

SESAME STREET

CTW

CHILDREN TELEVISIO WORKSHO

During World War II, British intelligence learned of a Nazi plot to kill **Prime Minister Winston Churchill** with exploding **chocolate bars.**

WOMEN ARE MORE SUSCEPTIBLE TO "CONTAGIOUS" YAWNING THAN MEN, A STUDY FOUND.

BLENNY FISH ESCAPE PREDATORS BY CRAWLING ONTO LAND.

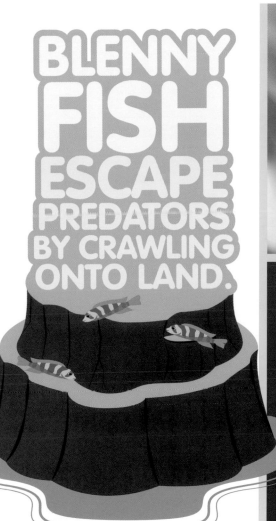

The **seeds** of some **trees** cannot **sprout** unless they are exposed to **fire.**

A COLLEGE STUDENT IN JAPAN CAN **SNAP HIS FINGERS 296 TIMES** IN **ONE MINUTE**—A WORLD RECORD.

YOU CAN BUY A WEARABLE TENT THAT FOLDS UP INTO THE HEEL OF A HIGH-TOP SNEAKER.

moggy= British slang for "cat"

A MAN IN BRISTOL, U.K., SNEAKS OUT AT NIGHT AND CORRECTS THE GRAMMAR ON SIGNS AND STOREFRONTS.

The amount of **chocolate** that **Belgium** produces each year weighs as much as **110,000 hippos.**

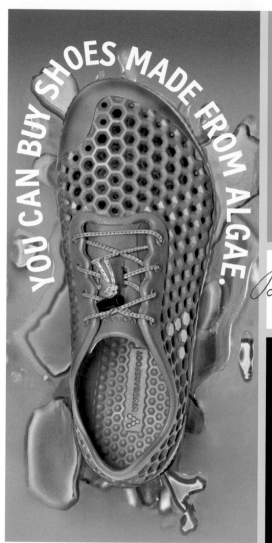

YOU CAN BUY SHOES MADE FROM ALGAE.

In 1738, a priest in France built a simple robotic duck that could eat—and poop out—a corn kernel.

Ben Franklin wrote a poem for a dead squirrel.

A PORTUGUESE MUSICIAN **CAN HIT A SINGLE PIANO** KEY A RECORD-SETTING **824 TIMES** IN **ONE MINUTE.**

In **World War II**, the U.S. used
inflatable tanks and **rubber**
airplanes to **fool** the Germans.

Police in California, U.S.A., found a man trapped in the chimney of the house he was trying to burglarize.

AN ALABAMA, U.S.A., COLLEGE STUDENT HAS MOWED 50 LAWNS IN 50 STATES — FOR FREE.

Some **ants** carry **umbrellas** made of **leaves.**

More than **half the world's tree species** are native to only **one country.**

Scientists made **bricks** from **Martian soil.**

One type of **gecko** has tear-away **skin** that helps it **escape predators.**

PREHISTORIC GUINEA PIGS WERE AS BIG AS COWS AND HAD A BITE AS STRONG AS A TIGER'S.

IN **ANTARCTICA,** HURRICANE-STRENGTH **WINDS** CREATE A RARE SCALY FORMATION CALLED "**DRAGON SKIN**" **ICE.**

The first English settlers to what is now North Carolina, U.S.A., **disappeared**, and no one knows what happened to them.

ORANGE PEKOE TEA CONTAINS NEITHER ORANGES NOR ORANGE FLAVOR.

IN 1958, CANADA **BLEW UP** AN **UNDERWATER MOUNTAIN** TO ALLOW SHIPS TO PASS THROUGH A CHANNEL.

A famous comedian donated more than **85,000 pages** of jokes to the **U.S. Library** of Congress.

IN TAIPEI, TAIWAN, COMMUTERS CAN RIDE A CITY BUS DECORATED WITH MOSS-COVERED SEATS AND LOCAL PLANTS.

THERE ARE RIVERS AND LAKES UNDER THE OCEAN.

A **shark** *photobombed* a 10-year-old Australian **surfer.**

CHIRPS=

CHIPS MADE WITH DRIED CRICKETS

THE "**GREEN FLASH**" IS A PHENOMENON IN WHICH THE SUN BRIEFLY CHANGES COLOR ON THE HORIZON AS IT RISES OR SETS.

THE BALL ON TOP OF A FLAGPOLE IS CALLED A TRUCK.

ONE STORE SELLS A PAIR OF JEANS COVERED IN FAKE MUD FOR $425.

Two ARTISTS in London, U.K., **BUILT A** maze MADE OF 250,000 BOOKS.

A BLACK **BEAR** BROKE INTO A HOME IN COLORADO, U.S.A.— AND **BANGED** ON THE FAMILY'S **PIANO**!

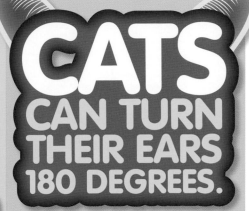

CATS CAN TURN THEIR EARS 180 DEGREES.

Martian meteorites have landed on **Earth.**

AN AFRICAN **ELEPHANT'S** DAILY AMOUNT OF **DUNG** CONTAINS MORE THAN 3,000 **SEEDS.**

You can buy a banana holder for your bicycle.

The town of Aladdin, Wyoming, U.S.A., population of 15, sold at auction for $500,000.

Nightingales can **sing** as loudly as a chain saw.

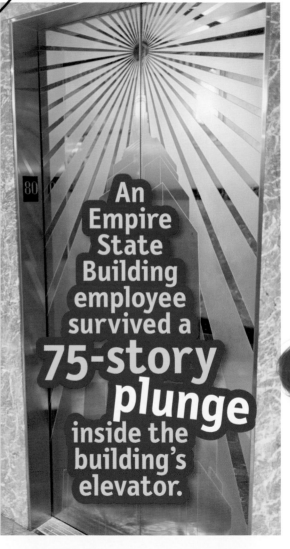

An Empire State Building employee survived a **75-story plunge** inside the building's elevator.

A NARWHAL USES ITS LONG TUSK TO STUN ITS PREY.

U.S. president *Thomas Jefferson* sometimes **wore a bathrobe** *when meeting with foreign diplomats.*

Air Force One contains a **mini-hospital** and an onboard **doctor.**

A **woman** in Florida, U.S.A., has a record-setting **collection** of 793 flamingo-related items.

Owls **cough up** a **pellet** packed with their **prey's** undigested feathers, bones, and fur **every day.**

YOU CAN BUY SALT & PEPPER SHAKERS THAT LOOK LIKE MAGIC WANDS.

During World War I, women knitted coded MESSAGES into scarves for fellow spies.

FOUR THOUSAND YEARS AGO, THE EGYPTIAN PYRAMIDS WERE SHINY AND WHITE.

FIVE COUNTRIES IN THE WORLD ARE ON TWO DIFFERENT CONTINENTS.

Africa and Europe are only nine miles (14 km) apart at their closest point.

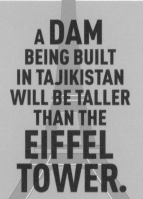

A **DAM** BEING BUILT IN TAJIKISTAN WILL BE TALLER THAN THE **EIFFEL TOWER.**

IT COSTS 19 CENTS TO PRODUCE A $50 BILL.

Ancient Romans sweetened their food with sugar made from lead.

Almost half the **gold** mined on **Earth** comes from one place in **South Africa.**

SCIENTISTS CREATED CYBORG PLANTS THAT CONDUCT ELECTRICITY.

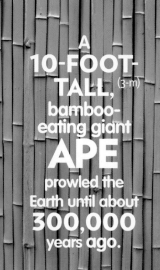

A **10-FOOT-TALL**, (3-m) bamboo-eating giant **APE** prowled the Earth until about **300,000** years ago.

A Chinese construction **CREW** demolished **19 BUILDINGS** in just **10 SECONDS.**

There are **125 MILLION 10-YEAR-OLDS** around the **WORLD.**

It takes about **10 DAYS** TO MAKE **PICKLES** out of FERMENTED **CUCUMBERS.**

RED **M&M'S** WERE **BANNED** FOR 10 YEARS.

The number **10** WAS SACRED to **PYTHAGORAS,** A FAMOUS ANCIENT **GREEK** MATHEMATICIAN.

THERE ARE 10 HUMAN BODY PARTS THAT HAVE JUST **THREE LETTERS:** eye, ear, leg, arm, jaw, rib, hip, gum, toe, and lip.

NINE out of **10 COUNTRIES** have at some point been invaded by Britain.

Paleontologists discovered a **PREHISTORIC**

SUPERCROC

that was as long as a
CITY BUS and may have
weighed as much as
10 TONS.
(9 t)

That's Weird! ...

The original
ROMAN CALENDAR
had only **10 MONTHS.**

IT TOOK **10 MINUTES**
FOR A COMPETITIVE EATER
TO **gulp down**
62 HOT DOGS.

A **MAN** in South Carolina, U.S.A.,
claims to have been
STRUCK BY LIGHTNING
at least **10 TIMES.**

A **BLINK OF AN**
EYE LASTS ABOUT
1/10 OF A
SECOND.

10
-TASTIC
FACTS!

127

A jaguar's **bite** is strong enough to dent a bowling ball.

Saying **"ow"** after you've been **hurt** may help you **tolerate pain,** according to a study.

A man was **stung mid-flight** by a **scorpion that had stowed away in an overhead bin.**

A **pizza shop** in Oregon, U.S.A., sold **slices** layered with more than **100 types** of **cheese.**

YOU CAN SPEND THE NIGHT IN A DOCKSIDE CRANE— AND EVEN OPERATE THE CRANE.

A BUILDING IS DECORATED WITH CONCRETE EMOJIS.

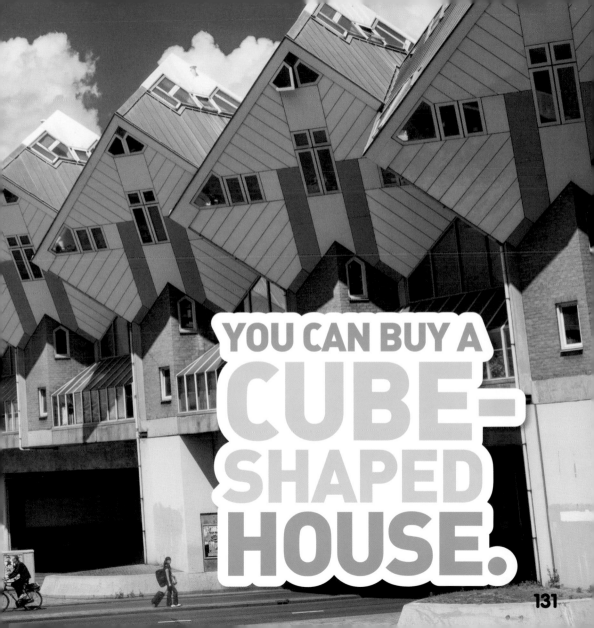

YOU CAN BUY A CUBE-SHAPED HOUSE.

TOADS DON'T HAVE **WARTS—** THOSE BUMPS ARE **SKIN GLANDS.**

A **101-year-old man** became the **oldest** tandem **skydiver** by leaping out of a plane **15,000 feet** above the ground. (4,575 m)

(1.2-m)

THIRD GRADERS IN NEW JERSEY, U.S.A., DISCOVERED A FOUR-FOOT-LONG **BOA CONSTRICTOR HIDING IN THEIR CLASSROOM.**

The world's **oldest** bookstore— in Lisbon, Portugal— has been open since **1732.**

ANCIENT ROMANS MADE PURPLE DYE OUT OF BOILED SEA SNAILS.

One man spent **two months** making a **church** entirely out of **snow** in a remote village in Siberia.

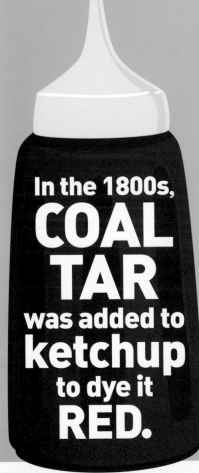

In the 1800s, **COAL TAR** was added to **ketchup** to dye it **RED.**

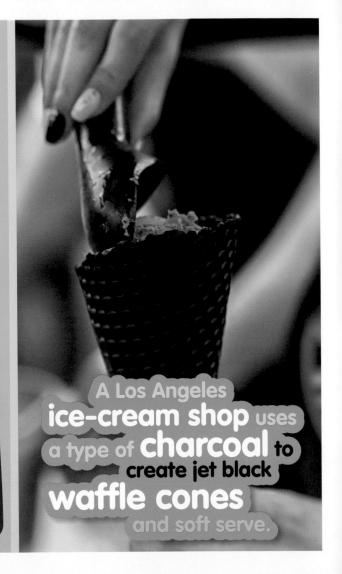

A Los Angeles **ice-cream shop** uses a type of **charcoal** to create jet black **waffle cones** and soft serve.

A New York man once bowled **12 straight strikes** in 86 seconds.

A U.S. ASTRONAUT SET A RECORD BY SPENDING MORE THAN 535 CONSECUTIVE DAYS IN SPACE.

You can tell a **whale's age** by counting the **waxy layers** in its ears.

CAMBRIDGE UNIVERSITY IN THE U.K. HIRED A "PROFESSOR OF PLAY" TO STUDY LEGO PLAYING AMONG KIDS.

THERE'S A SECRET **BASKETBALL COURT** INSIDE THE MATTERHORN RIDE IN **DISNEYLAND.**

whee!

MOTHS LEARNED TO DRIVE A ROBOTIC CAR.

MORE THAN HALF OF THE **LONDON UNDERGROUND** TRAIN SYSTEM IS **ABOVEGROUND.**

Hyenas like to roll around and play in their own **vomit.**

A VETERINARIAN AND HIS SON SPENT SIX WEEKS LIVING LIKE BADGERS ON A HILL IN WALES.

TINY BALLS OF FUNGUS AND MOLD CAN GROW IN YOUR SINUSES.

All mammals take about 12 seconds to poop, according to a recent study.

A **12-foot-tall** *model* of the (3.6-m)

Washington Monument

is **hidden** *in a manhole*

near the **monument** *itself.*

A message in a bottle floated in the ocean for more than **108 years before washing up** on a beach in Germany.

A rare white humpback whale was spotted swimming off the coast of Sydney, Australia.

A CEMETERY IN SLOVENIA SELLS TOMBSTONES WITH DIGITAL SCREENS TO SHOW VIDEOS AND SLIDE SHOWS OF THE DECEASED.

THE **SCREENS** HAVE A MOTION SENSOR AND **TURN ON** WHEN SOMEONE IS NEARBY.

One company **dyes** its clothing with a mixture of silkworm **poop**, dried **beetles**, and **food waste.**

Pop star Taylor Swift accidentally released **eight seconds of static** on iTunes— and it became a **number one hit.**

IT TAKES FIVE YEARS FOR A SPACECRAFT TO TRAVEL FROM EARTH TO JUPITER.

EACH YEAR, THE WORLD'S SPIDERS EAT AN AMOUNT OF INSECTS EQUAL TO TWICE THE WEIGHT OF THE HUMAN POPULATION.

Astronauts grow vegetables in space.

LEECHES STORE THEIR VICTIM'S BLOOD FOR MONTHS AFTER A MEAL.

Some nudibranchs, a type of sea slug, can store algae in their bodies to collect energy from the sun.

A U.S. FAST-FOOD COMPANY IS TRYING TO SEND A CHICKEN SANDWICH INTO SPACE.

STONE AGE HUMANS HAD EARLY VERSIONS OF DENTAL TOOLS FOR TREATING CAVITIES.

One type of **bacteria** can repair **cracks** in **concrete.**

From 1928 to 2013, the letters **Q, W, and X** were banned in Turkey.

A secret message was discovered in Abraham Lincoln's pocket watch.

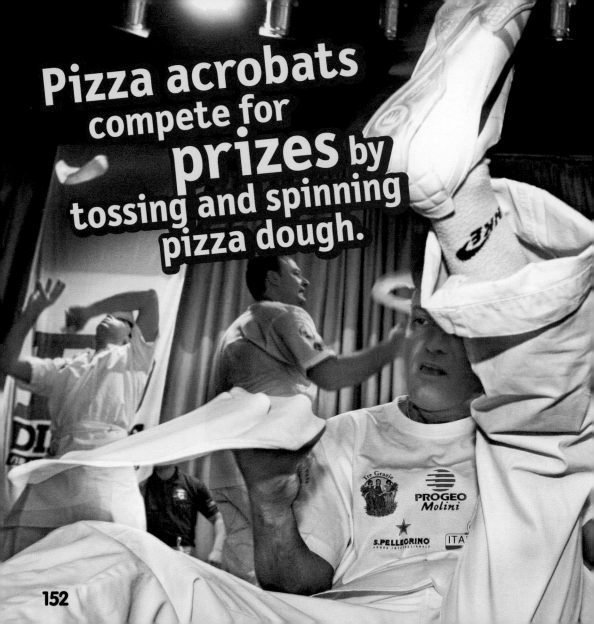

Pizza acrobats compete for **prizes** by tossing and spinning pizza dough.

More people snap **selfies** in the city **of Makati** in the Philippines than in any other place in the world, according to one study.

SCIENTISTS **BUILT** NANOSCALE CARS THAT CAN RACE ON A ROAD **THINNER** THAN A HUMAN HAIR.

A woman once married the Eiffel Tower after falling in love with the iconic Parisian landmark.

154

MORE THAN
20,000
RATS
ARE
WORSHIPPED
AT A
TEMPLE
IN INDIA.

A DOG

IS LISTED AS AN EDITOR OF A

MEDICAL JOURNAL.

IN 2015, EIGHT FEET **OF SNOW FELL** ON THE TOWN OF CAPRACOTTA, ITALY, IN ONE 18-HOUR SPAN.

(2.4 m)

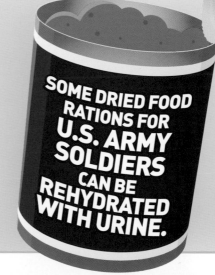

SOME DRIED FOOD RATIONS FOR **U.S. ARMY SOLDIERS** CAN BE REHYDRATED WITH URINE.

William Shakespeare
"*William Shakspere*"
"*Willm Shakspere*"
"*William Shakspeare*"
spelled his name
several
different ways.

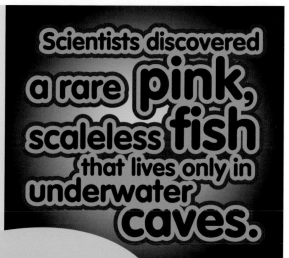

Scientists discovered a rare **pink,** scaleless **fish** that lives only in underwater **caves.**

AFRICAN ELEPHANTS SLEEP ONLY TWO HOURS A DAY, ON AVERAGE.

CORNSTALKS IN NEW YORK, U.S.A., GREW AS HIGH AS A FOUR-STORY BUILDING.

A woman in the U.K. claims she can **predict the future** by reading **asparagus tips.**

Legend has it that anyone who removes a *stone* from the *island of Koh Hingham* in Thailand will be

cursed.

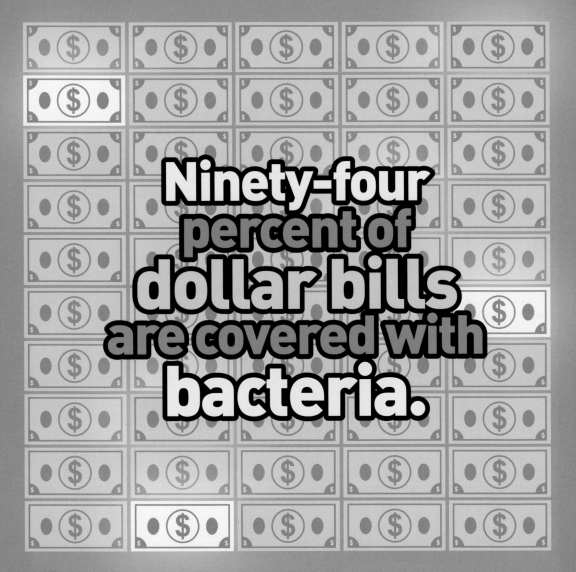

Ninety-four percent of dollar bills are covered with bacteria.

BlessU-2, a robot priest in Germany, can deliver blessings in 7 languages.

About **10 PERCENT** of land on Earth is covered with **GLACIAL ICE.**

FLEAS that infested **DINOSAURS** were **10 TIMES AS LARGE AS** today's fleas.

CRUSTACEANS with **10 LIMBS,** like crabs and lobsters, are also known as **DECAPODS.**

The **10TH PIN** IN BOWLING may have been added to get around laws that forbade **9-PIN** BOWLING.

THE WORLD RECORD FOR THE **WOMEN'S 100-METER DASH** IS **10.49 SECONDS.**

The average **CHRISTMAS TREE** takes as long as **10 YEARS** to GROW.

An Austrian man set a world record by completing **29 BACKWARD SOMERSAULTS** in **10 MINUTES** while wearing **SKIS.**

ABOUT **10 PERCENT** OF THE WORLD'S FISH LIVE ON **AUSTRALIA'S GREAT BARRIER REEF.**

The **MOON** is
238,855 MILES (384,400 km)
away—about the same
distance as traveling around
the **EARTH 10 TIMES**.

There are
**1.9 BILLION
$10 BILLS**
in circulation
around the U.S.

10 -TASTIC FACTS!

At a **RACE** in the U.K.,
RUNNERS complete
10 MARATHONS IN 10 DAYS—
that's **262 MILES!**
(422 km)

ABOUT EVERY **10 DAYS,**
YOUR **TONGUE**
REGENERATES ITS
TASTE BUDS.

That's Weird!

One in 10 PET **DOGS**
have their own
SOCIAL MEDIA accounts,
according to a
recent survey.

ITCHING IS CONTAGIOUS.

A **pop-up restaurant** in a California, U.S.A., dungeon offered customers a chance to **dine with rats.**

For $49.99, visitors to the Rat Café could eat while being surrounded by the rodents.

Theodore Roosevelt was saved from an assassin's bullet by a 50-page speech in his pocket.

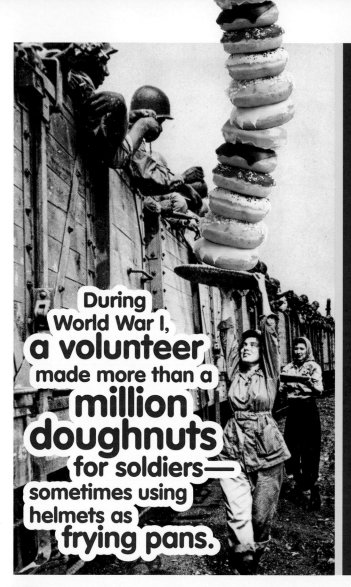

During World War I, **a volunteer** made more than a **million doughnuts** for soldiers— sometimes using helmets as **frying pans.**

A RUNAWAY PIG BLOCKED TRAFFIC FOR AN HOUR ON A BRIDGE IN MARYLAND, U.S.A.

A TERMITE QUEEN LAYS THOUSANDS OF EGGS EVERY DAY— MORE THAN A QUARTER BILLION IN HER LIFETIME.

A **VOLCANIC ERUPTION** IN INDONESIA ONCE MADE **SUMMER TEMPERATURES** IN CANADA DROP SO MUCH IT SNOWED.

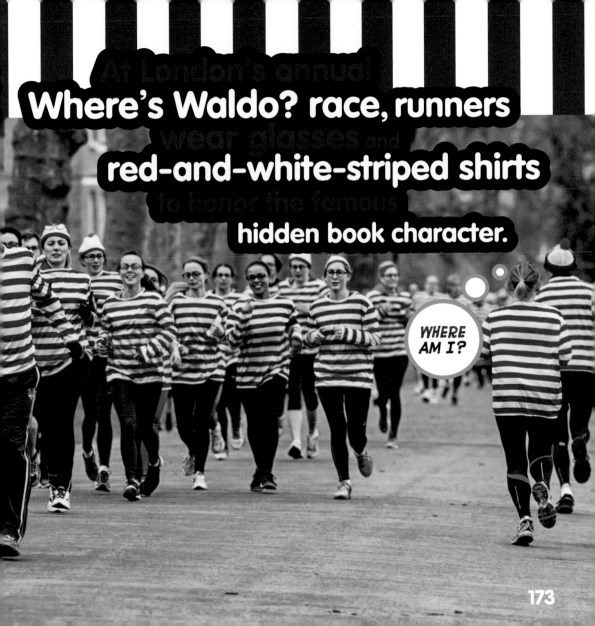

At London's annual **Where's Waldo? race, runners** wear glasses and **red-and-white-striped shirts** to honor the famous **hidden book character.**

WHERE AM I?

Paleontologists found a fossilized rat skull the size of a hippopotamus.

whoa!

A FORMER BRITISH SOCCER STAR SET A WORLD RECORD BY POSING FOR 134 SELFIES IN JUST THREE MINUTES!

ONE BRIDE AND GROOM RECENTLY HAD **SEVEN** WEDDINGS IN SEVEN COUNTRIES IN 40 DAYS.

TO TRICK POTENTIAL **THIEVES**, **SQUIRRELS** SOMETIMES PRETEND TO BURY A NUT.

A university in Georgia, U.S.A., has a collection of more than 1,000,000 ticks.

IN LESS THAN 15 MINUTES,
CAMELS CAN DRINK
ENOUGH WATER
TO FILL A BATHTUB.

An Italian company grows **strawberries** and **tomatoes** in **undersea** greenhouses.

The first **dinosaurs** with **wings** couldn't **fly.**

WEALTHY RUSSIANS HIRED FAKE AMBULANCES TO GET THEM THROUGH MOSCOW'S TRAFFIC JAMS.

There's a **swimming pool** shaped like the **state of Texas** in Plano, Texas, U.S.A.

IN JAPAN, YOU CAN HIRE A PROFESSIONAL TO APOLOGIZE FOR YOU.

Bandits have stolen millions of dollars' worth of nuts in California.

ARTIFICIAL-INTELLIGENCE RESEARCHERS HAVE CREATED SOUNDS THAT NO HUMAN HAS EVER HEARD BEFORE.

The planet **KELT-11b** is **larger than Jupiter** but has the **density of a Styrofoam ball.**

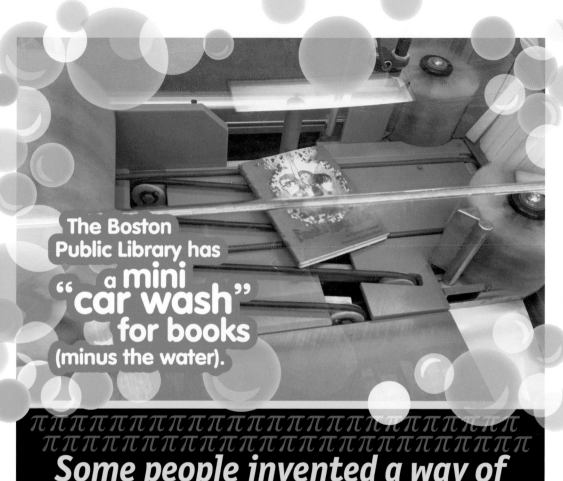

The Boston Public Library has a **mini "car wash"** for books (minus the water).

Some people invented a way of writing based on the number pi.

George Everest **never saw** the **mountain** that was named after him.

HELLO
my name is

GEORGE

Penguins the size of a **12-year-old kid** waddled around Earth **61 million** years ago.

In Sweden, there is a **bakery** and a cheese-and-cracker shop made just for **mice.**

NOIX DE VIE

Turiststråket

SWEDEN HAS ITS OWN NATIONAL FONT, SWEDEN SANS.

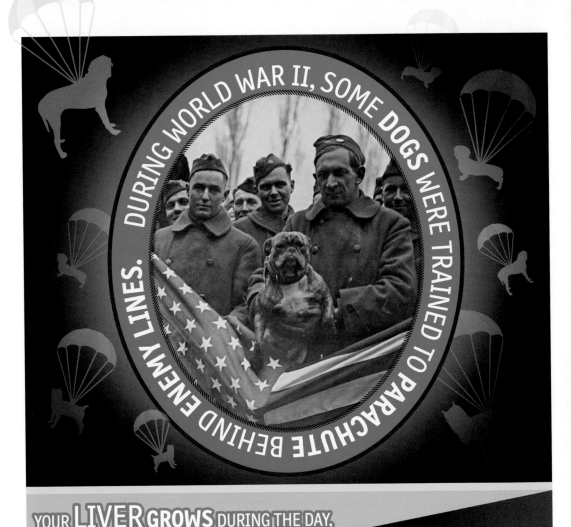

DURING WORLD WAR II, SOME DOGS WERE TRAINED TO PARACHUTE BEHIND ENEMY LINES.

YOUR **LIVER GROWS** DURING THE DAY, THEN **SHRINKS** AT NIGHT.

A medieval town sits at the bottom of a lake in Tuscany, Italy.

SOMEONE FOUND A 400-YEAR-OLD SHOPPING LIST UNDER THE FLOORBOARDS OF A HOUSE IN ENGLAND.

A Russian psychotherapist tried to hypnotize the entire Soviet Union by television.

Tortoise beetle larvae cover themselves in their own **poop** for protection.

Babies as young as **17 days old** can laugh.

A HUMPBACK WHALE'S SONG CAN LAST AS LONG AS 20 MINUTES AND IS OFTEN REPEATED FOR HOURS.

A Japanese artist made a **pair of shoes** that looked like **pigeons** so the birds wouldn't be **afraid of her.**

AN 18-YEAR-OLD RUNNER COMPLETED A HALF-MARATHON WHILE WEARING RUBBER SANDALS.

HE SAYS HE **RUNS** ABOUT **65 MILES** PER **WEEK** (105 km) WEARING THE **RUBBER SANDALS.**

A DAY ON THE PLANET VENUS IS LONGER THAN A YEAR ON VENUS.

Abstract **paintings** done by a four-year-old **dog** sell online for about **$40** each.

A **restaurant** in Michigan, U.S.A., serves a **hamburger** that weighs more than **300 pounds.**

SPIDERS BUILT A 98-FOOT (30-m) WEB IN A NEW ZEALAND FIELD.

The "ice" in the first ice-skating rink was made of fat and salt.

pee-ew!

GLACIARIUM.

(It smelled, and the rink closed in less than a year.)

Ears are self-cleaning.

Scientists turned a spinach leaf into human heart tissue.

A MAN IN AUSTRALIA BUILT A HOUSE OUT OF GARBAGE.

202

Fields
wildflowers
bloomed
from space.

You can order a **Kobe beef and lobster taco** for **$25,000** at a restaurant in **Los Cabos, Mexico.**

THE **DISH** ALSO FEATURES A **GOLD-FLAKED TORTILLA, CAVIAR, AND SALSA** MADE FROM A RARE **COFFEE.**

J WAS THE LAST LETTER ADDED TO THE ALPHABET.

In an **Alaska**, U.S.A., **neighborhood,** the street is a **runway,** and each house's " **garage** " is for an **airplane.**

Some bats can eat more than half their body weight in insects every day.

ABOUT
75 PERCENT OF ALL OCEAN

ANIMALS GLOW IN THE DARK.

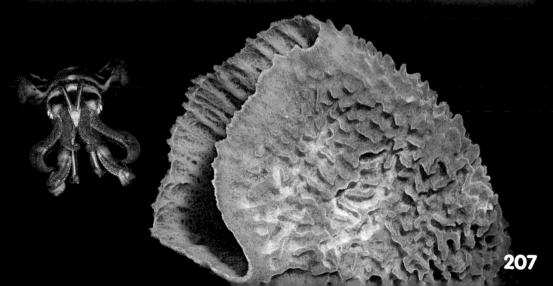

GUESS WHAT!

Here are nine MORE wild and wacky Weird But True books. (That's a total of 3,500 outrageous facts!) Collect 'em all!

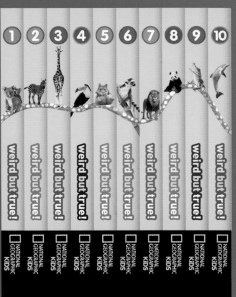

AVAILABLE WHEREVER BOOKS ARE SOLD
Discover more at natgeokids.com/wbtbooks

FACTFINDER

Boldface indicates illustrations.

A

Africa 122, **122**
African elephants 114, 157, **157**
Air Force One 117
Airplanes 97, **97**, 129, **129**, 205, **205**
Aladdin, Wyoming, U.S.A. 116
Algae 96, **96**, 148
Alphabets 45, 151, **151**, 205
Amazon rain forest 85, **85**
Ambulances 181
Antarctica 104, **104**
Ants 100, **100–101**
Apes, prehistoric 126
Apologies 181
Arizona, U.S.A. 66
Armadillos 18, **18**
Art 26, **26**, 84, **84**, 112, **112–113**, 196, **196–197**
Artificial intelligence 182
Asparagus tips 159, **159**
Astronauts 136, **136–137**, 147

B

Babies 49, **49**, 50, **50**, 64–65, 65, 76–77, **76–77**, 192, **192**
Bacon 43, **43**
Bacteria 62, **62**, 151, **151**, 162, **162**
Badgers 140, **140**
Banana holders 115, **115**
Basketball 84, **84**, 139
Baths 33, **33**, 66, **66**
Bats 12, **12**, 45, 205, **205**
Batteries 62, **62**
Bears 114
Beef 85
Bees 12, 15, **15**, 27, 68, **68**
Beetle poop 144, 190, **190–191**
Belgium 94, **94**
Bicycles 115, **115**
Big Bird 82, **82–83**
Black bears 114
Blenny fish 91, **91**
Blinking 127
Blood, stored by leeches 147
Blue whales 75
Boa constrictors 132
Boars 52, **52–53**
Boaty McBoatface (vessel) 30
Books
    giant 44, **44**
    maze made of 112, **112–113**
    number of 19, **19**
    oldest bookstore 132, **132**
    tiny 86, **86**
    washing 183, **183**
Bottles, messages in 141, **141**
Bowling 84, **84**, 135, **135**, 164, **164**
Bricks, from Martian soil 102, **102**
Buildings 126, **126**, 130, **130**
Bumblebees 12, 68, **68**
Burglar, stuck in chimney 98, **98**
Buses 106–107, 107
Butter 22–23, 23, 34–35, **35**

C

Calendars 127
Camels 177, **177**
Canada 105, 171
Cars 139, **139**, 153
Caterpillars 78, **78**
Cats
    attending high school 9, **9**
    British slang for 92, **92**
    ears 114, **114**
    on houseboat 14–15, **14–15**
    as perfume scent 37
    purring 74
Cell phones 7, **7**
Cemeteries 144, **144**
Charcoal 134, **134**
Chess 75, **75**
Chewing gum 26, **26**
Chicken bouquets 42, **42**
Chicken McNuggets 72
Chickens, sweaters for 81, **81**
Chimneys, burglar stuck in 98, **98**
Chimpanzees 58, **58–59**
Chocolate 90, **90**, 94, **94**
Christmas trees 164
Church, snow 133, **133**
Churchill, Winston 71, 90
Clothes 79, **79**, 84, **84**, 92, **92**, 111, 144

FACTFINDER

FACTFINDER

FACTFINDER

PHOTO CREDITS

Since 1888, the National Geographic Society has
funded more than 12,000 research, exploration,
and preservation projects around the world.
The Society receives funds from National
Geographic Partners, LLC, funded in part by
your purchase. A portion of the proceeds from
this book supports this vital work. To learn
more, visit natgeo.com/info.

For more information, visit nationalgeographic
.com, call 1-877-873-6846, or write to the
following address:

National Geographic Partners
1145 17th Street N.W.
Washington, D.C. 20036-4688 U.S.A.

Visit us online at nationalgeographic.com/books

For librarians and teachers:
ngchildrensbooks.org

More for kids from National Geographic:
natgeokids.com

For information about special discounts
for bulk purchases, please contact National
Geographic Books Special Sales:
specialsales@natgeo.com

For rights or permissions inquiries, please
contact National Geographic Books Subsidiary
Rights: bookrights@natgeo.com

Designed by Rachael Hamm Plett, Moduza Design

Trade paperback ISBN: 978-1-4263-3187-9
Reinforced library binding ISBN:
978-1-4263-3188-6

The publisher would like to thank Avery Hurt,
researcher; Sarah Wassner Flynn, researcher;
Grace Hill Smith, project editor; Paige Towler,
project manager; Kathryn Robbins, art director;
Hillary Leo, photo editor; Lori Epstein, photo
director; Joan Gossett, production editor;
and Anne LeongSon and Gus Tello, production
assistants.

Printed in Hong Kong
22/PPHK/6(SC)
22/PPHK/4(RLB)